Clara Lucas Balfour

Confessions of a Decanter

Clara Lucas Balfour

Confessions of a Decanter

ISBN/EAN: 9783743341609

Manufactured in Europe, USA, Canada, Australia, Japa

Cover: Foto ©ninafisch / pixelio.de

Manufactured and distributed by brebook publishing software (www.brebook.com)

Clara Lucas Balfour

Confessions of a Decanter

CONFESSIONS OF A DECANTER.

BY MRS. CLARA LUCAS BALFOUR.

LONDON: S. W. PARTRIDGE, 9, PATERNOSTER ROW.

THE CONFESSIONS OF A DECANTER.

CHAPTER I.

> "Let meaner clay contain the limpid wave,
> The clay for such an office nature gave.
> Let China's earth, enriched with coloured stains,
> Pencil'd with gold, and streaked with azure veins,
> The grateful flavour of the Indian leaf—
> Or Mocha's sunburnt berry, glad receive;
> The *sparkling Crystal** claims more gen'rous use,
> And mine should flow with more exalted juice."
> MRS. BARBAULD's "*Groans of the Tankard.*"

EVERYBODY acknowledges that this is the age of universal intelligence, I really, therefore, can see no just reason why a clearsighted, sparkling, radiant personage like myself, accustomed to *reflection*, as every observer can testify, should not glow with the spirit of the age, and become a candidate for literary fame; particularly as I have the advantage of age and experience, and have observed through a clear, not an

---

* A slight alteration has here been made from the original words of the poem quoted.

opaque medium, many changes in men and manners—opinions and customs, since I was first fashioned by a skilful London workman, and made one of a goodly row of brethren, that were ranged in glittering order round the shelves of a noted glass-shop, in one of the leading thoroughfares of the metropolis.

Perhaps some reader may exclaim, "I like autobiography, but then the narrator must be a personage of substance, and have some brains, or how can I attend?"

Alas! my good friend, depend on it, I am not the first hollow, brainless personage, that ever presumed to trespass on thy attention and crave a patient hearing; and as for substance, who ever heard of authors being people of substance? Have not that race, time immemorial, been celebrated for a delicate transparency of texture that enabled knowing folks to see through them quite easily? Have they not often been the receptacles of spirits more potent than the outward frames that contained them—spirits, that when once suffered to escape, have proved perfectly inflammable? Have they not also been frequently found more ornamental than useful, more brilliant than durable? Have they not often had to endure a fiery ordeal in a hot furnace of affliction, before they were fused into the given form that carping critics required; and what crystal is ever *cut* more elaborately than the poor author, by that stern and capricious lapidary, poverty? And then, every one knows that when he has at length attained that frail and brittle thing—a reputation, doubtless, to him, a perfect prism of gorgeous sparkling beauty; from some unexpected quarter, a rude blow is dealt, and an unsightly flaw, or leaky crack is inflicted, or even worse than that, perhaps the poor author's fame is shivered to atoms; and who cares to note, that the fragments are glittering, or who stretches out a hand to pluck them from the mire of oblivion? Yes, undoubtedly, there are many points of resemblance between me and the author tribe, therefore, there is, I trust, the less presumption in my taking up, without any farther preface, the office of narrator of my own history.

I have before stated, that my earliest recollections extend to the fashionable and well-stocked shop, where I glittered in company with many others. I may venture to speak of my appearance without vanity, for as beauty depends on taste, I am no longer noted for my comeliness, as I was in days of yore,—my shoulders being too round—my neck too thick, and my head-gear (commonly called, my stopper) too high and pointed for modern taste. Nevertheless, I cannot entirely forget that I was once thought beautiful, and surely this is a pardonable weakness for I have undergone no change, and many a lady of my acquaintance who has altered in every feature, on the strength of having once been beautiful, thinks herself privileged to be vain and capricious to the end of her life, and ill-tempered with all the world for not yielding the homage with which she was first greeted.

It was in the middle of a fine summer's day, when the sunbeams danced merrily in our shop, and threw over, or drew out of us such lovely flashes of green and gold, crimson and azure, that the rays seemed to thrill with delight, when a young lady, charming as the day, entered, leaning on the arm of a pleasant sturdy-looking gentleman in a naval uniform. There was not many years difference in their ages, and I soon discovered by the happy way in which the lady kept saying '*we*,' as if the plural number was just then a charming novelty with her, that they were man and wife, and but recently united. "I think *we* want that, shall *we* have this? *We* will order those," and many similar expressions, showing the unity of their connubial bliss. The husband assented gaily for some time, to all demands, evidently looking more at his wife's bright, happy face, than at the sparkling crystals around. They ordered several handsome ornamental things, and still the lady seemed to look about, as if the pleasure of buying were too great to be easily relinquished, when there was a slight admonition in the tone in which the husband said, "My dear, you have now, I think, all that will be required, at present."

Just at that instant, the bright eyes of the young wife were raised to the shelf where I was glittering.

"Oh dear, what beautiful decanters, how very elegantly ornamented!" she exclaimed.

In an instant, I, and a half-a-dozen more, were taken down and placed before her.

"Oh," said the husband, "there are plenty of those things at home, you will find abundance there, depend on it."

"Oh, but dear Robert! they are all so old-fashioned, —not a modern decanter or glass in the house. Come, you *must* grant me one favour, just a pair of these elegant decanters and a dozen of wine glasses cut to match."

"Well, well, make haste and choose them—we shall be too late if we linger any longer here."

The lady having thus gained her point, chose me and my counterpart, and suitable glasses, then leaving their address—a neighbouring hotel—and ordering their purchases to be carefully packed, as they were going out of town, they departed.

"What a charming couple," said my master's eldest daughter, following them with admiring eyes up the street, "how happy they look!"

"Aye, aye, Nancy," replied her father, "early days yet, my child, they've all their troubles to come, poor things!"

"Oh, father! how you talk about troubles, I'm sure such a sweet young lady, and such a fine, good-natured, manly-looking gentleman, make one quite happy to look at them,—what have they to fear?"

"Why everybody, my girl, has cause to fear; happiness in this world is such a breakable commodity, and nobody knows how soon a crash may come,—but you young folks think it a fine thing to be married."

"Oh, father!" exclaimed Nancy, colouring indignantly at such an exceedingly unlikely charge, "how can you say I ever think of such a thing!—I've made up my mind to keep single."

"Oh, no doubt you have, my dear, and you'll keep to that till the right person asks you to change your mind, certainly you will."

Nancy put an end to the conversation by scampering out of hearing of her father's dry quaint raillery, and I, and my companions, being duly packed, were sent to our destination at the hotel, and from thence, judging by the motion, made a long journey, with the particulars of which, I shall not trouble the reader, being cooped up in darkness, which to persons of my nature, is unfavourable to reflection.

I, and my companions, emerged to light at last, and found ourselves in a comfortable old-fashioned country-house. The bells of the village church rung a merry peal in honour of the arrival of my master and mistress, who, I soon discovered, were returned from making a wedding tour that had occupied three months; I also learned that my master was a Lieutenant in the Navy, an only son; and that his father whose house we were now in, was the Squire, and lived in the Manor House of the Parish of Nettlebrook.

The old gentleman had been long a widower, and it

was agreed that his son's bride should come home to the Manor House to live, as her husband's profession called him away; and the aged father and young wife, were to be a mutual comfort and protection to each other, when the hope and stay of the family—the young naval officer, was absent.

Squire Rubicand, was a most portly old gentleman,—rosy in the face, and amazingly fat in form; but at the same time very helpless: indeed, prematurely decrepid. At the time of our arrival, one hand was enveloped in flannel, and supported by a sling, while the other rested upon the stick, with the aid of which he supported and regulated his somewhat tottering and infirm steps.

Of course, there was a great rejoicing when the newly-married pair arrived. The young lady laughed and wept almost at the same time, as old Squire Rubicand welcomed her home. The village gentry, which in that remote district, consisted of the doctor, lawyer, and their wives, and Mr. Meek the curate, were all assembled in the drawing-room. Two servant maids and one man were running briskly about, and smiles seemed to sit on every face, except one, and that gloomy exception was the comely middle-aged person, who first unpacked us in her snug room, and who I found had long been housekeeper in the establishment of the Squire. She took us out of the hamper with a jerk, set me down on the table with a violence quite distressing to my nerves, and kept muttering at intervals, "I'll be even with them." "That little farthing-faced chit is not coming here to be mistress over me, I can tell her;" and many similar observations, from which I was led to infer that she feared her long-continued sway over the household was at an end, and she was jealous accordingly. I noticed that when we were unpacked, and dusted, and placed on a little tray, that the housekeeper went to a cupboard, took a drink out of a black bottle, looking carefully round towards the door, then wiping her mouth, cut a piece of lemon peel, and began munching it preparatory to going upstairs, whither we accompanied her. She proceeded to a very neat dressing-room, commanding a noble prospect of hills towering in the distance, fringed with woods that partly overhung a pretty winding, rapid stream, which descended from the hills and flowed through the broad green valley that spread before the house. The bride was standing at the window admiring the view, when the housekeeper with a somewhat stealthy tread entered the apartment, and curtsying very low, with many smiles and civilities began to speak to the young lady, who turning her open countenance and cheerful smile full upon her, answered her inquiries in regard to her health, and whether she had found everything in the order she wished, &c.

"I am quite glad, Mrs. Specious," said the young wife, "that I am to have an experienced person like you with me, for I am so new to my duties, that I should feel quite unequal to them if it were not for the prospect of your assistance; you know Mr. Rubicand's habits so well, that I intend to profit by your experience."

This conciliatory speech was answered by the utmost obsequiousness from Mrs. Specious, who, observing that the young lady looked pale, began sympathizing with her, and recommending some restorative, adding—"Do, my dear lady, let me get it for you!" A reluctant negative was languidly uttered by Mrs. Rubicand, which the housekeeper interpreted in her own way, by going out and speedily returning with a bottle and glass, the former containing what she called an 'elegant cordial' of her own making—a sovereign remedy against low spirits, langour and fatigue. The temptation was effective, the young lady took the potion, and condescended to admire the flavour, when Mrs. Specious proposed to fill me with the contents of the bottle, and place me in a little cabinet that stood in the corner, to be ready for use when any emergency occurred.

Just as this arrangement was completed, the husband of my charming mistress entered, and fondly chiding her delay, led her down to the drawing-room.

Meanwhile, Mrs. Specious put me in my place in the corner as cabinet-minister, muttering as she did so, "Ah! ah, I shall know how to manage my lady—only let her get fond of '*drops of comfort*,' and she'll not be hard to rule; I'll have everything my own way then."

CHAPTER II.

> "I have told,
> O Britons! O my brethren! I have told
> Most bitter truth; but without bitterness.'
> Nor deem my zeal factions, or mistim'd;
> For never can true courage dwell with them
> Who, playing tricks with conscience, dare not look
> At their own vices. We have been too long
> Dupes of a deep delusion!"—COLERIDGE.

IT may be thought that surveying so small a place as the corner were I was stationed, I could not have a very extended view of affairs, but like other cabinet-ministers, I was taken into the secret councils of many in the family—indeed, I soon found myself an object of secret attention. My kind young mistress was too young and guileless herself to suspect others, and she never thought of placing me under lock and key; the consequence was, that Patty, the housemaid, when she finished dusting the room, used to take a little of my contents, saying, as she wiped her mouth, "What's good for the mistress is good for the maid." And fat Dolly, the cook, if ever she looked into the room, when all was still, used to take a similar freedom, saying, "It's hard if poor sarvants as toils all day, mayn't have a little of what some folks has too much of;" and as for my mistress, she found the flavour of the cordial I contained, very pleasant; and she felt so revived after taking me, that, being in delicate health, Mrs. Specious prescribed two glasses daily,—one at eleven o'clock in the morning, to produce an appetite, and one the last thing at night, to procure sleep. My readers must observe that I held a medicine not a beverage, though I confess I could not understand the distinction, —for there were several bottles of medicine standing in a recess near to my station on the cabinet, but they were undisturbed by any secret admirers. And if on any occasion they were wanted, there were such wry faces made, and such hesitation exhibited, that I concluded I held a very different sort of compound, being always in request and constantly replenished. One thing, however, troubled me much, for I often saw that when Patty, or Dolly, or Mrs. Specious, or indeed my mistress herself, had taken a draught of my contents, they were always somewhat different—and often far less agreeable in their manners than they had previously been. It seemed to bring out whatever evil they had in their dispositions. It made Patty invariably pert and talkative. It sent Dolly downstairs cross and quarrelsome, and Mrs. Specious always used to appear so dreadfully tender and affectionate, so ready to flatter and cajole, so able to weep, or smile, as it suited her, that she seemed almost as subtle as the very Evil-one himself, whom I had heard them read about; while my mistress, after her morning dose, would sit down languidly on the sofa, in a kind of easy, indolent abstraction, unfit and unwilling for any useful employment.

Before a month had elapsed, my young master's leave of absence had expired, and he set off to join his ship—to the no small grief of both, doubtless, but especially to my mistress—for the grief of those who stay in quiet and leisure, is always of a different kind from those who go to scenes of activity and bustle.

A sense of loneliness settled with deep depression on Mrs. Rubicand's spirits—and my power became more confirmed than ever—for when she would not have thought of me, Mrs. Specious would pour out a glass and hold it to her, tempting the rosy lip to taste, and then when the soft eyes kindled with the fire the draught supplied, and the delicate cheek mantled with a flush of heat, she would say, "Now, my dear lady, you look better, I can see that has done you good."

Mrs. Rubicand was gentle, amiable, and benevolent; but alas! fond of ease, and Mrs. Specious with the famous cordial for her auxiliary, soon contrived to rule her entirely. One day when Mrs. Rubicand went down to the village, which she very seldom visited—to my surprise, Mrs. Specious and the old Squire entered together, the latter hobbling, as if his infirmities were rapidly increasing. "Pray sit down and rest here," said the housekeeper—"'Tis too much for you to go downstairs all at one stretch."

"I suppose Specious," said the Squire, "that my daughter likes this room with the lovely view it commands, for she spends a good deal of time here." "Bless me," he added, sitting down exhausted, "how tired I feel."

"Do try a little of this," said Mrs. Specious, producing me, "'Tis my mistress's *favourite* cordial." In an instant a glass was in the old gentleman's hand, and he drank it with evident relish.

"That's very strong, Specious!" he said—and then remarked thoughtfully, "My daughter-in-law is young to have adopted a *favourite* cordial, and of such strength too."

"Oh, poor lady, she is so low-spirited, and this quite keeps her up, she is very fond of it."

"Indeed!" was the reply, in no very pleasant tone—then recollecting that he had left his snuffbox in an adjoining room, he desired Mrs. Specious to fetch it, muttering to himself as she departed, "An infirm person like me, undoubtedly requires stimulants; but it is quite another thing for a young lady, just a wife, and soon to be a mother, to give way to such indulgence. Ah, dear! that's quite another matter."

It was evident that suspicion was aroused, and an unpleasant prejudice created—from that time my mistress grew more low-spirited than ever, and more self-indulgent. Mrs. Specious reigned with undisputed sway over the household, and also over the young mistress, whose health seemed to be fast becoming as uncertain as her spirits, and the cordial I supplied, was more than ever in request. Nervous fears, violent hysteric fits, alternated with wild bursts of puerile mirth. Oh, the change a few short months had wrought in the gay and graceful, the amiable and lovely woman, whose face when I first saw it, seemed the very picture of happiness. From the fatal time when I had been the innocent instrument of mischief, by imperceptible, but sure degrees, she had altered for the worse. Mourning her husband's absence, she had allowed herself to change in every respect from what she was when she won that husband's love; and instead of combating grief with active employment, sank into careless unavailing despondency; while her indolence made her rather a burthen upon, than a companion to, her father-in-law; who, whatever might be his own failings, was sharp-sighted enough to discern those of others.

While affairs were in this state, the house was one day suddenly the scene of great confusion. A portly old dame took up her abode in the adjoining bedroom—and she had not been long installed in her office, before she found me out, tasted and praised my flavour, protesting, however, that she never took either spirits or wine, but that an elegant cordial like that I held, was quite innocent.

THE INFANT'S OPIATE. [Page 15]

My life was now very monotonous, for all I heard was the wailing cry of a little infant, who seemed constantly fretting. This poor little pining being was not many days old, when the old lady I have named, brought it into the dressing-room, and gave it a spoonful of my contents, a little diluted, "There, little cross-grain, that'll make you sleep I hope," said she; then, hearing a feeble voice, I knew to be my mistress's, calling from the bedroom, she said, carrying in the half-stifled child, "Oh, bless its precious heart—the lovely angel—it looks so much better—bless it." From that time I was in request for mother and infant; not much to the benefit of either apparently, for many weeks went by, and my mistress still laid, overcome with a slow nervous fever, on her couch, and the babe was always fretting, unless stilled by my liquid into a sort of stupor. There was a wet-nurse there, who, strong and healthy, refused to touch my contents, vowing that when she once tasted it, her mouth was burnt; and who seemed to keep up her strength on a very simple diet; while her child (nursed in the village by a poor woman, who lived principally on porridge and potatoes,) was fat, rosy, and good-tempered, and presented a marked contrast to the little withered, fretful babe, who being a son-and-heir, was an object of great importance—and alas, of great infirmity. How it lived on, so restless and unhappy, I know not, except that a naturally strong constitution was aided by a healthy nurse—still the daily dosing was never thought to be the cause of evil, but was clung too by both mother and child, as the panacea for every ailment.

A slight variation in the aspect of affairs occurred, when news arrived that the naval officer, now promoted to the rank of Captain, was coming home for a time, to see his wife and little son. The poor listless invalid rallied to receive him—the old Squire, though now confined to a wheel-chair by his constant plague—the gout, rejoiced in the news; and every plan, but the right, was tried to improve the health and appearance of the infant—that is, the cordial was not discontinued, and all other measures were neutralized by its power.

No words can describe the grief depicted in the countenance of Captain Rubicand, when he beheld the fearful change that little more than a year had made in the blooming girl he had left—all the tenderest sympathies of his heart were called forth, as well they might be, for the unhappy, but still charming victim of alcohol, though he little guessed the source of her disorder.

CHAPTER III.

"Death is less terrible than living torment—
Estrangement from one's self is death indeed;
A banishment from those we truly love
Is self from self."—SHAKESPERE.

I SAID that old Mr. Rubicand had taken a prejudice against the young lady who owned me. He had in fact, been greatly disappointed in his son's marriage; and as the wife he had chosen, was a portionless orphan, it was thought she would exert herself, to please the family she had entered. The old Squire was an indolent man, and wanted amusement,—a vain man, and needed admiration—a lonely man, and craved for society; in all these desires he had been disappointed. A feeble invalid had been added to his household, and that was the only change that had been effected—the Squire, therefore, had adopted a melancholy phraseology, in speaking of the affair, calling it his son's 'unfortunate marriage;' and this tone was generally adopted by the little circle who shared in the joys, sorrows, and scandal of the Manor House.

Mrs. Rubicand slightly rallied, it is true, on her husband's return, but the *incubus* of habit was not to be thrown off easily, and she was not the person to make the effort. Indeed, she looked upon me as her great auxiliary in the work of rousing herself, and in the hope of being more cheerful, increased her daily dose; then, under the influence of the excitement that I supplied, talked gaily, and in truth, foolishly,—exerted her fluttered spirits, and returned to her chamber exhausted, feverish, cross, and hysterical. Meanwhile, her excitability was commented on, and a key to the cause of it was found in the increase in the wine-merchant's bill, which Mrs. Specious, now that her plans were so successful, took care to present to Squire Rubicand. Alas! what a change soon took place in the husband. He became dissatisfied, suspicious, irritable, severe,—domestic happiness was gone, and how could she, who knew not how to preserve it when all was fair, hope to lure it back, now that it had been so completely exiled from the roof?

It occurred to me as I stood in the cabinet, in that unhappy lady's room—an unsuspected cause, and a reflecting witness of all the misery that was suffered there, that nothing in this world is produced spontaneously, but evil. Angry tempers, pernicious habits, spring up with speed and vigour, like sturdy weeds, and flourish abundantly; but goodness, peace, domestic joy,—oh! these want care and cultivation. Self-denial, watchfulness, industry, cheerfulness—these are the virtues that enrich the domestic circle, and produce refreshing fruit and lovely flowers.

Well, things went on from bad to worse rapidly. It's mighty easy to go downhill, everybody knows. The poor drugged and stimulated infant became, if possible, more cross; the house was unbearable, and the child's nurse, feeling that she had not the sole charge of the child, and suspecting the cause of its crossness to be the *remedies* which were administered, gave the family a choice of evils, either to let her leave, or to give her the child at her own home. Contrary almost to her expectations, this latter plan was agreed to by Captain and Squire Rubicand joyfully, while the poor nervous mother was scarcely consulted. She felt keenly how powerless she had become in her own home—how slight a hold she had on her husband's relaxed affections, and though she might still have his compassion, respect and esteem were at an end. Then came artifice. I was no longer filled with the cordial Mrs. Specious made, nor stood in my accustomed place; but by means of bribing Dolly, the cook, I was filled with brandy and locked up in secrecy, to be often visited by the poor infatuated victim. Meanwhile, I heard in my prison, voices telling that the child had recovered; and wicked tongues darkly hinted that the visits of Captain Rubicand to his child, were made really, more to its nurse. My mistress's intellects were so confused, that she gave heed to any scandal, and coming one evening to me for support, drank my remaining contents—a draught quite enough to prostrate reason, hastily put on her shawl and bonnet, and left me on a table by the window, from whence I observed her cross the lawn and take the road to the nurse's cottage, on the banks of the stream opposite our house, where (after prying into the window) she entered.

It seems, her child was sleeping in the cradle, while the nurse had for a moment gone upstairs. Intent on gaining possession of the infant, in the vague desire of asserting her rights, or of contradicting her husband, she took the sleeping babe in her feeble arms, and hastened as fast as her trembling limbs would bear her, towards her home. But she had not proceeded far, when just where the bank of the river was steepest, her unsteady footsteps failed, and the next moment she was in the middle of the current struggling for life. The infant fell from her grasp, and its heavy clothing absorbing the water, it soon sank, while the miserable mother buffeted in the shallows, and was overwhelmed just as the nurse, who at length saw her from her upper window, rushed forth and gave the alarm. Some minutes elapsed before they could be rescued—minutes that were nearly fatal to the mother, and quite so to the babe. It was some time before the former was restored to consciousness—alas! only to comprehend the full misery of her situation. The accidental, yet in some sense, wilful author of her child's death,—this was the awful climax! Her husband cold before, was now utterly estranged; her own heart was her most severe accuser; those who taught her the habit that had ruined her, were loud in her condemnation. On earth no consolation remained, and to heaven she did not look—I doubt if she knew how; for though in the house there was a sort of profession of religion, yet if much was displayed, there was very little of it kept privately, as stock in hand.

Where there is a good wine-cellar, and numerous dinner parties, and a Squire, rosy in the face and gouty in the hands and feet, religion is oftener talked about than seen or practised.

But to return to the poor self-condemned culprit. Her reason previously impaired, was shattered by the fearful events of that night; for weeks she lay unconscious, then her disorder changed, she recovered her health under a strict and simple regimen, but the mind was all but gone. Her disorder settled in confirmed imbecility, and the last time I saw her, she was playing with an infant's rattle, and singing nursery doggrel (the only thing she remembered) to an imaginary baby. The nurse or keeper who attended her, was kind and gentle, and the poor victim was moved from the Manor House and placed permanently under her care. The Captain went off to sea—a stern man whom sorrows had hardened rather than subdued. The week after his departure, Mrs. Specious, more to the annoyance than the surprise of many, became the wife of the Squire, who, drivelling in the dotage of intemperate old age, was capable of any folly.

An event like this caused a revolution in the family, that affected even me. The new mistress played the lady with a high hand; and though Dolly for love of ale and ease, bore it contentedly, Patty, the pert housemaid, having one day a mingling of the spirit of contradiction and the spirit of wine, tossed her head, and told the bride that she should leave, and hoped in her next place to serve her betters! Oh, the mutterings, grumblings, and smashings that took place, between the time of Patty's warning and her going!

Being one day altering and arranging the dressing-room, now used by the new lady, she flirted her duster with such vengeance, that my companion, who stood near, went down with a crash. A thought seemed to strike Patty. Gathering up the fragments, she seized me, and saying, "Well! Ma'am Upstart has no right to these; if she'd any conscience, she could not bear the sight of the poor young lady's decanters, and I may as well be hanged for a sheep as a lamb,' besides, I don't pay for breakage." So my companion was broken into a multitude of pieces, and I was carried upstairs, and snugly deposited in Patty's box. I never doubted that she made out that we were both broken.

The next day I found by the motion that we were travelling, and the artful Patty, and the box in which I reposed, towards night, arrived at a small tinman's shop, in the quiet street of a neat little town. I was soon unpacked for fear I might be broken, and I found the master of the shop was Patty's brother. He looked a very different person from his sister. Honesty was written on every line of his open face, and attested by every corn on his hard and brawny hands. There was a troop of sturdy little ones, merry as skylarks, though not quite so musical, and a healthy, happy-looking woman, whom the tribe hailed as 'mother;' and whose name seemed never to cease being called for something or other. The place, though fresh and tidy, was certainly by no means smart. It was new to me to find myself set upon a wooden dresser, among delf platters and brown pitchers; surrounded by windsor chairs, an oak table and a Dutch clock. Strange to say, I could not perceive one decanter in the place, and yet the people looked quite contented.

CHAPTER IV.

"O long may Heaven their simple lives prevent
From luxury's contagion weak and vile,
Then, howe'er crowns and coronets be rent,
A virtuous populace may rise the while,
And stand a wall of fire around our much loved isle."
       COTTER'S SATURDAY NIGHT.

"I do love to see Mrs. Kitty dance,
She swims about like a piece of butter in a frying-pan."
       HIGH-LIFE BELOW STAIRS.

I FOUND that the family I was at present introduced to, differed from that I had quitted in many other particulars than those of mere outward circumstances. Patty, on the strength of having just left a gentleman's family, determined to show her gentility and superiority to her relations, and therefore treated them to many of the secondhand airs and graces, which I had often seen practised by her before the looking-glass. Strange to say, the good people of the house were quite undazzled at the display of her grace and dignity; indeed, her brother smiled compassionately once or twice, and his artless, unsophisticated wife, in the midst of her friendly hospitality, felt such pity for the temptations and delusions which she thought Patty must have been surrounded by, that her folly seemed to her mind only the natural consequence of youthful vanity and dangerous associations. They were, in truth, very primitive people, for soon after our arrival, the good man of the house looked at the clock, and saying, "it was time," summoned his little family,—an evening hymn was sung, a chapter of the Bible was read, the family all joining by turns in the reading, and then a prayer in simple fervent phraseology, was offered up by the husband and father of the household. After this the little ones went off to rest, and the elders conversed awhile on different topics; and if the language was homely, and the pronunciation rustic, there was a tone of good sense pervading it, which struck me as very different from all I had heard in the dwelling of the Squire; and I perceived that though there was no decanter besides me in the place, that there was a little set of book-shelves hanging against the wall, containing about thirty volumes of books. Pre-eminent among them, standing next the Bible, I saw one called "The Life of John Wesley." During my subsequent stay, I found that the life, labours, and writings of this good man, were, next to the Bible, the chief intellectual refreshment of the family; and though I discovered that this same John Wesley was no friend to decanters, and perfectly hated their usual contents, I am bound to say, that a more happy, orderly, sensible household, than this family of his followers, it was impossible to see. Patty, poor thing, was soon tired of the place,—" What a hum-drum set," she yawningly muttered one night, when the room was for a moment empty. One of Patty's greatest privations in her brother's dwelling, was the entire absence of strong drink—they actually drank *water!* with their meals; and when she spoke against it, her brother said, "Strong drink of every kind is an unnecessary, indeed a pernicious luxury. A poor man with a large family, who wishes to provide things honest in the sight of all men, has no money to spare for luxuries. My wife and I never drank any spirits, and we gave up everything but small beer, years ago, and at last we gave up that, for it was no good; we've done quite as well without it, and the money that the quarterly cask of table-beer used to cost, I have to spend in books. "There they are," he added, glancing with honest pride at the shelves. " Food for the mind, Patty, that is far better than the bread that perisheth, and not to be compared with strong drink of any kind; and in John Wesley's life I find such encouragement to persevere in water-drinking, that I would not change my plan for anything."

" I thought, brother, that though you were a Wesleyan, you only followed your founder in your religious matters. He might know plenty about piety and all that, but what did he know about other things?"

" A sensible, learned, thoughtful man, was John

Wesley," replied he, "who spent a very long life in doing good,—who laboured from youth to old age every day, and all day long—who travelled into many regions, and saw human beings in many stations—must have had great experience, and could not fail to know the best way of living in this world, as well as the best way of gaining an inheritance in the better land. He was a worker and a thinker—an observer and a preacher; and if I follow his leading in the mighty matters of my spiritual well-being, shall I not trust his judgment in the far less important matters of my temporal good?"

"Oh! but other Wesleyans don't do that."

"No, many do not, but I never can understand their receiving his testimony on greater matters, and rejecting it in the lesser, but still weighty concerns of this life. But let others do as they please, *I*, and my house, *we* will follow, to the best of our ability, his personal, as well as his spiritual example."

Such kind of conversation, and such habits of living were not by any means to Patty's taste; and just as she was getting very impatient, she heard that a London lady, who had been staying in the neighbourhood of the town for her health, was going back to the metropolis, and wanted to take a servant up to town with her. Patty's brother thought that it would be well, as the lady was quite a stranger (known to no one in the town), to make some inquiries about her, before Patty went with her to such a place as London. But his sister was eager to go, and relying on her own judgment, which was infallible in her own opinion, she pronounced Mrs. Hague "quite the lady, not a dowdy country hum-drum, but gay, smart, and Frenchified," and all arrangements were speedily concluded.

Patty had managed her money so badly while at the Squire's, that she had none left to buy the children anything in return for living at her industrious brother's frugal home. Ashamed of the meanness that is ever the companion of extravagance, she thought of giving me to her sister-in-law, saying to herself, that as I cost her nothing, it would be a cheap way of returning the obligation; so having made up her mind to this stretch of liberality, she presented me at the breakfast table on the last morning of her stay, but to her chagrin, her sister, poor homely creature! said, "No, thank you, we don't want anything of the kind, I like things all of a piece—and a fine cut-glass decanter would be out of place, and make my other things look quite shabby; besides, it would be of no use; we are not ashamed of being water-drinkers, every one that knows us, knows that; and if we were to get on ever so, I should never think of buying such a thing—no, we are better without it, I'd rather not take it, Patty."

"We are plain people as you know," added her husband, "and such like furniture is the last I should wish to see in my poor home; plain food, plain clothes, plain furniture, and plain education, while God gives me health I hope to earn, and to teach my children to earn after me; but if once the love of finery, in any form, takes possession of me or mine, it will throw all into confusion—no, no, Patty, you are very kind, but we 've been married eleven years, and done very well without a decanter, and we will try to do without one for the years that may come."

"Well, I 'm sure," said Patty, tossing her head and carrying me off in a pet, " some people ha 'n't got a bit of taste, and it 's no good trying to make a silk pus out of a sow's ear," with which elegant maxim Patty's remarks on taste concluded. To say truth, I was not sorry that the good man had rejected me. Considering how Patty became possessed of me, I was indeed unworthy to stand amid the honestly earned homely furniture of the dwelling. And his remarks were perhaps the more plainly spoken, that his sister might benefit by them, and not spend her money (as he thought she had in my case) on useless luxuries.

I was again packed up and carried first to the lodgings of Mrs. Hague, Patty's new mistress, and thence by the mail to London, where I soon found myself in a large house among plenty of gaiety. Patty for a little time was quite in her element—she was allowed to wear what she pleased, and as her mistress was somewhat careless and profuse in gifts, the means to be smart were in some measure added to the inclination. There was, to my mind, something mysterious in the new house and its mistress. There were two other servants, a man and maid, besides Patty, and they all seemed idle and luxurious. A char-woman came on the sly to do the house-work in the morning before the lady was up. The evenings were spent by the mistress, at places of amusement, and by the servants, at cards and drinking, and in receiving their acquaintances. There were not many visitors at the house to Mrs. Hague; indeed, only one—a gentleman, who came and went mysteriously. Patty slept in a room adjoining her mistress's, and I occupied a snug place in a glass corner-cupboard, near a middle door that separated the lady's bedroom from Patty's. I was filled with a compound called "Hodge's Cream of the Valley," but Patty put a paper label on me with "Camphor Julep" written in large letters, and perhaps, this false name was the reason that I stood there unmolested, except by Patty herself; and from this position I saw enough to convince me that the gaiety of the lady of the house was nothing but outward show. Poor wretch! how hard she toiled, and how much she suffered in the service of sin! Sometimes after hours of preparation, when her mysterious visitor was announced, she would pass by my station, looking so blooming and smiling, that it seemed as if she had never shed a tear in her life; all that art, and fashion, and dress, could do to heighten natural charms, or to conceal premature decay, was done, and to all appearance, successfully. But I saw both sides of the picture. The poor slave of dissipation would return from the opera, or the theatre, either unnaturally excited, or so languid, it was pitiable to behold her. Oh, the sleepless, troubled nights she had, rising often and walking the room—sometimes calling Patty, who slept near her, for the purpose of attending her. She suffered with horrible nervous pains in her face, and yet more with mental pangs; her sobs and groans were dreadful, and when morning came, what a meagre, wan, shattered creature, did it exhibit, as she lay till noon on her unquiet bed; obtaining at intervals a little unrefreshing sleep. Pillaged and unpitied by those who ate her bread, obliged at peril of losing the guilty luxury in which she lived to conceal her physical and mental misery,—to play the agreeable and exert herself,—to please one whose value for her was merely as being

"A toy for dotard's play,
To wear but till the gilding frets away."

That this poor toil-worn victim of sin and sorrow should drink, and often very copiously, seemed to me a natural part of her wretched servitude of Satan. I could better understand her doing so, than a woman of character polluting her lips with the fiery abominations of Alcohol.

Patty either was, or affected to be, very much surprised, when she was told the sort of lady she had engaged herself to serve. However, when her fellow-servants told her that it could not be helped now, and prophesied that Mrs. Hague "would n't last long," that she "was on her last legs, &c.," the hope of pillage, and the love of an easy life, with a mistress whom she might negligently serve and diligently cheat, reconciled her to the odium of her service. It is one of the miseries of guilt, that it is ever followed and served by bloodhounds that scent their prey afar off. "There is no friendship with the wicked." Oh, if there were no other punishment than this, surely it would be enough to prove, "That the way of transgressors is hard." At least, the miserable Mrs. Hague, pining in her lonely home, found it so—often when tossing on her pillow, would she exclaim, "Oh, that in this wide weary world there was one human being that really loved me!" Alas, she had found by bitter experience—

"That still to guilt occasion sends,
Slaves, tools, accomplices,—no friends."

CHAPTER V.

> "Here lies now a prey to insulting neglect,
> What once was a butterfly gay in life's beam;
> Want *only* of goodness denied her respect,
> Want *only* of virtue denied her esteem."
>   BURNS.
>
> "Can such things be—and overcome us like
> A summer cloud, without our special wonder?"
>   SHAKESPERE.

FROM my station in the corner-cupboard, I had ample opportunity of observing what an influence my contents had on the purposes of those who used them. Sometimes Patty would be seized with a qualm of conscience at the servitude she was in, and would tell her fellow-servants she had resolved to give notice and try and obtain a more reputable place. Sometimes, also, she would feel some compunction, at the heartless system of cheating that went on under a mistress, that none of them either feared, loved, or respected; while occasionally a feeling of compassion touched her for an instant, when she saw how sadly the poor slave of false pleasure, toiled to endeavour to appear cheerful; and what a dreadful reaction took place when her forced gaiety departed, and with none to witness she sank down into despondency, left alone with a guilty conscience and a shattered constitution. Yet it was only for Patty to take a draught of my contents, and these feelings fled quicker than they came; and her tongue could cajole and flatter, while her heart became as hard as the nether-millstone. Meanwhile, things were rapidly drawing to a conclusion with the wretched mistress of the mansion. Her feebleness and sufferings of the body—and also, doubtless, of the mind—began to alter her personal appearance. In vain art was resorted to, to supply bloom to the faded cheek. The eye became hollow and dim, and the graceful form, shrunk from its round and fair proportions, becoming as sharp and angular as it was tremulous and fragile. This change had been observed by one who valued her only for her poor fleeting beauty, and who resented its decay as a fault in her and an injury to him. "You positively look ten years older within these few last months," was his remark—then adding, "The races are next week, and I want you to look well and stylish then—for I don't want to be told I am driving an old woman with me, so see that you look better by that time."

These were hard conditions, and as the event proved, beyond the reach of the slave they were required from. The race day came, and violent spasms compelled Mrs. Hague to remain in her joyless home, while her indisposition provoked the anger, rather than roused the sympathy of the sinful man, for whom she had renounced all that makes life endurable.

By Patty's contrivance in the after-part of the day, I was refilled with her favourite " Cream of the Valley," my assumed name of Camphor Julep was still announced on my exterior, and during an interval in the paroxysms of Mrs. Hague's attack, I was introduced to her notice. As usual, my contents proved irresistible and overwhelming — mental misery and physical exhaustion combined to induce her to drink deeply—and very soon the remembrance both of sorrow and pain, had vanished, and she sunk down on her sofa in the deep lethargic sleep of inebriation. From this sleep the loud knock and heavy tread of her visitor, returned from the races, failed to arouse her. He entered, gazed upon her thin face, ghastly in its paleness—and turned away with a look of disgust, as her hot and tainted breath came upon him; then gazing round espied me—my assumed name was no protection, for he tasted my contents; a bitter smile came over his sarcastic features. "Oh, oh! if it comes to this, better end it all at once—a good opportunity perhaps," uttered he—then seating himself at a small writing table near, he penned the following note.

"You know my temper will not brook a rival, I have long suspected I had one, and this evening I found my rival lurking under an assumed name in your room.

There is certainly no accounting for taste, but I entertain too humble an opinion of my own powers, to attempt entering the lists against so formidable a rival as GIN, particularly as I never knew a case in which this important personage once encouraged, did not come off conqueror in the long run. I have determined therefore to say, farewell, and leave the field to my supplanter, any compromise of the matter is impossible, so give up the idea. Wishing you had shown a better taste—accept my adieus."

This note he so folded, that it would twine around my neck, where he fastened it with a seal, and departed, evidently glad of an opportunity to break with one he was tired of. Ah! this was sport to him; but death to her! His hand had calmly bound the heartless farewell round my neck; but even my cold surface glowed as the burning tremulous hands of Mrs. Hague, on awakening, tore the strange missive from me, and the well-known writing met her gaze. She read it over at first, without comprehending it, then sat for some minutes in a stupor—read it again, and felt rather than understood its import. A hollow groan burst from her pallid lips. She did not faint, but stood erect, and sobered. 'A *rival!*' she at length exclaimed, "Did he think I could ever have lived his slave, unless strong drink had helped me? Yes! it has helped me to live a guilty life, and now it *must* help me to die an untimely death, and the sooner, the better."

Such were the fearful reasonings of this poor perverted creature. A strange calm—a sort of stony despair settled upon her, petrifying both the conscience and the feelings. Patty came with well-acted obsequiousness, and offered her usual nightly services. They were declined. "I have letters to write, that will detain me up till a late hour, so you may go to bed."

Left to herself, she unlocked a small cabinet, and taking thence a little phial marked LAUDANUM, she looked intently upon it for a few minutes, and then saying, "I knew it must come to this, how often have I said, 'a little of this allays my spasms—a larger dose will cure all ills'—I rejoice that I'm thus prepared."

After sitting for some time in a kind of stupor, gazing on the fatal dose, she commenced writing; but apparently her pen refused to do its office as she wished, and as the night wore away, she destroyed the notes she wrote one after another. At length, impatient at her failures, she rapidly wrote a few lines, saying, "The rival you complain of was your faithful ally; like you it sparkled to deceive—it allured to destroy, betraying its victim with a kiss; like you, it is insensible to the misery it has caused. You introduced me to this rival, and that introduction gradually reconciled me to being —what I will not attempt to name, for no words can convey an idea of HER lot—who has madly given all— body and soul—*all!*—and found herself despised, derided, and deserted, in return."

After sealing and directing this, she took out several papers that looked like tradesmen's bills, and sighing heavily, attempted to form an estimate of their amount. In vain! the reeling brain refused the task, and the phial was in her hand and at her lips; but a yearning love of life yet clung to her heart. She looked around wildly, as if for escape, like a hunted deer at bay. The potion was put down. There yet remained a copious draught of the insidious liquor of temptation at my disposal, and, with the speed of thought, it was poured out and drank, then all reflection ceased, and with a wild exulting laugh—uttering her betrayer's name as a toast, she drank the poison! Staggering to her bed, she wrapt herself in a large and costly shawl, and the last words she uttered were in reference to this article of dress—" 'Twas *his* first gift, and 'twill now make my winding-sheet!"

The morning sun shone brightly into the chamber of death — hour after hour, and the deep breathing of the miserable woman gave place to short convulsive gasps; her pale cheek became more pallid. The large eyes, with pupils fearfully dilated, partially unclosed, and rolled about in the death agony, while cold damps gathered on the rigid brow, and the limbs writhed in the last struggle that nature made with its overpowering foe. It did not seem an easy death, for who that has felt the seemingly protracted misery of nightmare can doubt that in that mortal strife with over-mastering lethargy, there may be convulsive agonies not the less frightful, because they are never revealed? So, however, it seemed in the case of this miserable being, to judge by the changes that passed over her wan face, before the last gurgling sob was heaved, and the wretched spirit had quitted the tabernacle of clay, and left the region of life and hope for ever!

It was nearly noon (for in that house they kept late hours) ere Patty came to attend her mistress. I pass over the exclamations—the runnings to and fro, and all the talk that this matter occasioned. One thing, however, referring to myself, I am bound to mention, I never did so much work, as during the three days that elapsed between the death and the funeral. There was, of course, plenty of gossiping between the servants and their cronies, and equally, of course, they could not talk so glibly without my help. There was the inquest too, and then I was wanted to help the witnesses to give their testimony—which they did by the aid of my contents, by all solemnly swearing that not one of them knew the real name or residence of the man who had been her tempter and partner in guilt, though they knew very well, but gold had bought their silence. Then, also, I was chief mourner at the funeral, for I wept more copiously than anybody; indeed, all the tears that were shed I supplied. There's a class of people in London, who can distil gin into tears very quickly, such a class were the harpies that saw Mrs. Hague to her last home. I was also used alternately by all the servants, to give them nerve to execute deeds of plunder, on all that they could filch from the creditors. In particular, Patty felt afraid to approach the dead body, until a draught from me gave her courage, and then she could unwind the shawl the suicide had wrapped herself in, and fold it away for her own especial service—she did the same also with many things beside. Oh! aided by a decanter of spirits, there is no deed of darkness that need appal even the most timid!

Well, this life is full of changes; very soon after I wept at the funeral, it was my lot to sparkle at a wedding. Patty and the man-servant knew so much of the depredations each had committed, and were so dangerously acquainted with each other's affairs, that they had mutually the power to ruin each other. The man —a shrewd fellow, having a wholesome dread of Patty's malice, proposed marriage as the best way of making a possible accuser into an ally; and the vision of a home of her own was too captivating to be withstood by her. Thus they came together. Patty soon found her vision of a home was not likely to be realized, unless she could keep one, or rather, make one herself. There was some noisy mirth in the outset of the career of this guilty couple, but long before the honeymoon was over—disgust, hatred, and starvation, were all the household furniture they possessed, and these three I managed to

THE CONFESSIONS OF A DECANTER. 41

keep in the highest possible perfection. All the trinkets and clothes that Patty and her helpmate had purloined from the poor suicide, found their way, day after day, to the pawnbroker's—till at length these were exhausted: then came strife, blows, "confusion worse confounded." The brutal ruffian determined to have money, and that Patty should procure it for him, no matter how nefarious or odious the means she had to use. Tongue or pen can never describe the horrors of that winter to Patty—cold, hunger, insult, brutality! each in its most unmitigated form, was her portion. In four months from the day of her marriage, the smart, healthy, pert and giddy country girl, had become the most gross, squalid, noisome refuse of humanity, that ever the loathing senses recoiled from. Gin was food as well as drink to her; but no longer did I contain this favourite auxiliary of her trade. The means to procure enough to fill me, were beyond her reach. Pence earned by guilt, hid away from her rapacious husband, were immediately exchanged for the fluid of death thus taken in frequent doses

CHAPTER VI.

> "All night I lay in agony,
> In anguish dark and deep;
> My fevered eyes I dared not close,
> But stared aghast at sleep;
> For sin had rendered unto her
> The keys of hell to keep!"
>   THOMAS HOOD.

WHILE things were going all to the bad with Patty and her husband, it happened that I was permitted to pay a visit away from their abode, and if my nature had allowed me to feel as deeply as I could see things clearly, I must have mourned over the scene I was taken to. I've heard people say that some human troubles are enough to make the stones rise and testify, so there's no wonder that I, being of much more brittle form and texture, and fashioned by the hand of man, should make my reflections on his woes.

In the same house with Patty there lived a woman who was a sick nurse; she had been a night nurse at a neighbouring hospital, but was discharged, as she said, for nothing in the world else, "but taking a little drop to help her in her toilsome duties." which certainly seemed a hard case, as she represented it. Well, this woman was not without employment, for she was often sent for to attend cases of sudden illness, or to prepare the dead for the grave; and neither of these duties could possibly be rightly performed, without the aid of such spirits as I generally contained.

One night, when my mistress came home wet through and miserable, and had just thrown herself down on the truckle-bed, too tired to take off her clothes, there was a great knocking at the door. Patty jumped up, for she feared it was her husband, and when he came home making a thumping like that, on the outside of the house, it was a kind of preliminary to some "bad scrimmage," as our Irish neighbours called it, when he got inside. Shivering with fright and cold, Patty went to the door, and found there a sort of half-witted boy, who asked if Nurse Sippit lived there. The noise he had made roused the house, and the person he asked for was leaning over the balustrade of the stairs, listening, and now came forward saying, " Aye, my lad, here be Nus Sippit, right and ready for any one as wants her." The boy then urgently besought her to come to his mother's, Mrs. Grip's, for their lodger was dying— " and bring" he added, " some brandy with you, for see, I've broke the bottle," holding as he spoke, the neck of an ugly common green bottle in his hand.

" Ah, clumsy! that's jest like you—but you go back, and I'll be with your mother in a brace of shakes.'

A few minutes afterwards, Mrs. Sippit fully equipped entered our room, and asked Patty, who had laid down again, if she could lend her a bottle—"mine," she said, pulling a flat half-pint bottle from her pocket, "is such a skimping bit of a thing, it holds next to nothink."

As Patty was a sort of crony of this woman's, she rose, and looking on the shelf, where I stood, said, "I've nothing between one your size and this, Mrs. Sippit." Patty eyed me lovingly and added, as the nurse grasped me and said I would do very well. "Be careful of it, I ain't got much left of my good things now, but when I thinks of the many and many a drop of good stuff I've had out of this yere decanter, it goes to my heart to look at it, empty and all." With this, she began to cry, and Mrs. Sippit said, "What! down on your luck? my dear, come along a-me and have a drop."

Though my mistress had been so tired, that she could hardly stand, she roused up at this proposal, and instantly set off to the Wine Vaults, that stood at the corner of our row. Here I was more than half-filled with brandy, Mrs. Sippit taking a glass out of my contents, and Patty drinking a similar portion of gin. There were some women of their acquaintance at the bar, and Mrs. Sippit began to tell them, how she believed it was all over with Mrs. Grip's lodger—"I knows his case, I've nussed him, off and on, for some months." The young lady with gold earrings and hair rolled off her face, who had replenished me from a tap, seemed to take some interest in the statement, and said in a kind of mincing voice, being very genteel—

" Is Mr. Aspinly considered worse ? "

" He's as bad as he can be," was the reply.

" Humph! poor man, he's been a good customer since he came into this neighbourhood."

Just at that moment, Patty's husband staggered into the place, and went up to the bar, hiccupping out a compliment to the young lady, whom he called " My blossom!" when he suddenly noticed his wife, and aiming a blow at her, drove her, with oaths, out of the place. Mrs. Sippit taking no notice of what seemed a common occurrence, grasped me firmly in her hands, and went off to her patient.

I was ushered into the close and dusty-looking bed-room, of a sort of third or fourth-rate lodging-house There was a good fire in the grate, and before it a comfortable easy-chair, with plenty of cushions. At first, I thought the person in the chair, wrapped up in a large flannel gown, and fast asleep, was the invalid, but it proved to be Mrs. Grip, who, on being roused by our entrance, said peevishly; " I 'm tired to death, a-waiting here for you, Sippit; I ain't agoing to stay no longer for nobody."

The nurse seemed to understand the way to soothe this woman, for she instantly set me down on the table, and looking round for a wine glass, poured out a brimmer, and handing it over, said, " There, my dear, that 'll set you up; and now you go to bed, and I'll see and make all comfortable."

In a little time we were left alone, and I stood on the table, winking and glowing between the light of the candle and the fire, the bed was opposite me, and propped up in a half-sitting posture, was the strangest-looking object I had ever seen. It was a long time before I could make out all the details. A man, certainly not old, for his hair was still a dark brown, and straggled in a kind of tangled mass on his shoulders, mingling with a beard still darker, that fell round him like a mane. The face, all of it that could be seen for his shock of hair, was ghastly white, and worn to the very bone. But what most attracted me was the eyes—gloomy, large, deep-set, and glassy, and so filled with what seemed molten fire, that they appeared like two lamps shining out of their cavernous sockets. The nose was pinched, and the corners of the livid lips, as far as they could be seen for the beard, were drawn down. I saw that his chest laboured heavily, and the breath came in thick gasps. He was making signs with his hands, which Mrs. Sippit was too intent on her own personal arrangements to notice. At last she turned and looked at him, then took up the candle and drew near, and seemed to be taking the gauge of his strength. She put her hand on his head, and drew it back, covered with the damp that seemed to have saturated his hair. "Humph, he'll not last long," she said aloud. He

THE DYING DRUNKARD. (Page 47.

shook off her hand as she attempted to touch him again, and pointed impatiently towards me; the woman understood him, poured him out a glassful, and with a teaspoon in her hand, prepared to administer it, but with unexpected strength, he eagerly clutched the glass in his long, bony hands, and though they were very tremulous, by bowing his head forward, managed to drink off the potion at a draught. He sank back exhausted for a minute or two, and then spoke quite clearly, and with great rapidity.

"Nurse, has my sister come? Nurse, do you think me worse? No, no, I'm not worse! I'm getting better, I'm surely getting better! It was needless to send for Anne. Why, I feel much better, very much. Why do you look so at me, as if I were dying? I'm not dying, so don't croak, you old raven."

He was silent an instant, and then he shouted out, "Die! —Oh God, I dare not die! I must not, I will not die!" His voice rose to a scream. There was a sort of choking catch in his throat, that lasted full a minute. Then he caught his breath, and drawing it slowly for a few seconds, said in a hollow voice:—

"'After death, the judgment!' Ah, I have preached from that—yes, yes, I felt it then!" A rigor shook him until the bed trembled, and he shrieked out, "Felt it!— oh, I feel it now; 'after death, the judgment!' Then I'm dead—this is the judgment. It's here, Nurse! Water! The bed's on fire! Look at the flames! Water, I say!"

He rose upright with maniac strength, and stretching forward, fell heavily with his face on the footboard of the bed. The nurse seized a long towel, and running to him, passed it across his chest, and pinioned his arms. The gaunt form was so wasted, that the bones stood out rigidly, and seemed by their sharpness, to have worn the rents in his tattered nightshirt; for a minute these skeleton limbs struggled, then with a few convulsive heaves, he lay in a heap on the bed, gasping and powerless. With a good deal of rough pulling and grumbling, the woman dragged him back to the pillow, and then, seeing he was quite exhausted, she seated herself, and putting on a little kettle, began to make preparations for her own comfort. I, of course, was in request, and whether the sick man slept or not, Nurse Sippit dosed away heavily; the low moans of the sufferer, acting as a kind of lullaby.

At five o'clock in the morning, there was the sound of a vehicle coming to a sudden halt at the street door, and a bell was rung, gently at first. The sick man heard it, and turned with a weak, anxious gaze on his pillow. No one else heard it. The ringing was repeated again and again, and at length Mrs. Grip's son went shambling half-asleep down the stairs, and in a few moments footsteps were heard approaching; the room door opened, and a widow lady, attended by a youth of about fourteen entered. The two stood a minute, and saw at a glance the smouldering fire, the candle flickering in the socket, the snoring nurse, and the dying man. Yes—dying! the sands of life had nearly run out. With a strong effort at self-control, the lady approached the bed. "My dear brother," she said in a husky voice—"My poor dear brother." The youth, horrified, sunk down on his knees, hid his face in the bedclothes, and wept bitterly.

"Dear! who calls me dear? Oh, Annie, is it you?—go, go away child, this is no place for you. I'm dead and lost—for ever lost! 'After death, the judgment!' I'm very cold," he added, shivering. "There's cold torment, as well as hot! You know frost can burn—it's all torment!"

"My brother, cry to Jesus; think of Him! No, no, it's not too late; you are not dead! Call on Him. Oh, Lord, have mercy!—dear William, the thief on the cross said, 'Lord, remember me,' and was heard. Nurse, what is this? Oh James, call the nurse."

A gurgling sob came from the sick man—he tried to speak through his clenched teeth, his eyes wandered towards his sister; she clasped his hand, bent her head over it, as her tears fell fast. Suddenly there was a fixed stare, a struggle, and then a sort of ashy tint spread over the face, the jaw fell, and——

"He's gone," said the nurse, who had been roused by the youth—"He's gone! I wonder he lasted so long."

"My poor brother, this then is thy end! oh, my dear, dear brother!" The lady fell on the neck of the youth, who called her mother, and who, as he held her in his arms, said, "Oh, is he really gone—can nothing more be done for my poor Uncle?" The words "Nothing more," seemed like a dirge, and mother and son wept in silence.

Presently, Mrs. Grip, with her most obsequious manner, came into the room, and the mourners, looking at her and the nurse with terrified glances, as if they had never seen such women before, left the chamber of death for a time.

Then I became of great importance. Before either woman did any of the needful work to the poor skeleton before them, they finished my contents, and set me up on the top of a high press, where I could see without being seen, and then after an hour or so, they left the room, saying, "The 'Crown and Sceptre' is open by this time; send the boy there; this is thirsty work, and as they looks as if they can well afford it, we'll have what's proper—in course we will."

I had not been long left alone with the dead, when footsteps approached, and the door was gently opened, and with a hushed tread, and both weeping, the mother and son came to look on all that remained, of one they had evidently loved well. They stood together in silence for a time, then by one impulse, they knelt, and after a few minutes of silent prayer, the mother said, "Oh, Lord, help us poor feeble creatures to cleave to Thee; oh, keep us from the Tempter's snare; Jesus, Saviour of sinners, hear us; save us from trusting to ourselves, make us to feel that all our strength and safety is in Thee." Here sobs broke in and choked her utterance, and the youth, hardly less agitated, faltered out the one word, "Amen." They rose from their knees, and sat down together at the bedside. The lady seemed to be nerving herself for an effort—she was evidently struggling with her grief. The youth made as if he would lead her from the room. "Not yet," she said, at length with forced calmness, "My dear James, before I leave this room, I must tell you what I hope you will never, never forget. You have no father, and I must not allow this great grief to pass, without a solemn word to you. Here, in the presence of the dead, I must speak. My poor dear brother was, at your age, and for years after, one of the very best, and most gifted persons I ever knew. At school, at college, among friends, in his home, he was all that was dear and estimable. Ah! my boy, and he seemed to have the root of the matter in him, and all his gifts and graces appeared the flowering forth of true Christian principle. He entered the ministry. What he was in the pulpit, on the platform, you have heard and read. We loved him for himself, but oh, much more as a teacher of righteousness, wise to win souls."

"My dear son, how can I tell it, but the outline you must have heard. He fell. Yes! the allurements not of bad company, but of good society, proved too much for him. He studied hard, it was said he needed stimulants, kind hands offered them, oh, cruel kindness! kind voices wooed him to his ruin! A temperament less highly nervous, might have better resisted their effects. I'm not here to tell you the degrees by which he fell, but the fact. Yes! he fell, and then those who had been active to allure, were horror-stricken, and became as active to condemn. He left the place, not only a disgraced man, but a disgraced minister; feeling that he had 'crucified his Lord afresh, and put Him to an open shame.' But, though he left the scene of his once holy labours, and recent disgrace, he did not put away the cause of that disgrace. In feeble health, and loneliness, and sorrow, he yielded to the Tempter. His circumstances were bad. He began to write for the press. I should not dare tell you this, my son, if I had made no effort to rescue him. It was for his sake I signed the temperance pledge, and wrote to him, and came again and again, before he sank to such a dwelling as this. Alas! in vain. Your dear father's long illness impeded my efforts; my brother drank more and more I was told. We lost sight of him altogether for a time. Now and then, I recognised his hand in the articles I read in one of the Magazines, but even in these, the manner was altered. Gloomy views of life, dreary doubts, or cynical strictures, were all that the fine intellect, once so instinct with hallowed fire could give,—this ceased. Your dear father's death was seen by him in the papers, and he wrote to me a wild, strange letter, I answered it, and then came this week, a wretched blotted scrawl, calling on me to come, for he was dying. I don't wonder at your grief my boy, so recently as you have stood at your dear father's death-bed. Ah, there, all was peace and joy. Here! Oh, my poor William! Promise me, my boy, that God helping you, you never will enter into that temptation, that has been his ruin, and the ruin of thousands—myriads! Oh, be humble, my James. Do not think that you can stand in the slippery paths, where so many of the wise and good have fallen."

"Dear Mother, I do promise that I will pray to be enabled to walk in the steps of my father and yourself."

"As far, my son, as we have followed Christ, who denied Himself for us."

Just then, the misery of the scene she had witnessed, seemed to come over the mourner with overwhelming force, and the youth took her weeping bitterly from the room, and I saw them no more. I was taken by rough hands, back to my former quarters,—not, however, long to abide there,—other changes were soon in store for me.

CHAPTER VII.

*"King Alcohol's slaves passed out and passed in,
Ragged and woe-worn, shivering and thin;
And though differing in form, the eye could trace,
A signet of grief, stamped on every face."*
KING ALCOHOL'S WALK.

ONE day, when an empty cupboard and fireless grate, added to the rigour of the frost without, and the squalor within our dreary dwelling, Patty's eager-looking eyes fell on me, and a sudden thought seemed for a moment to give energy to her famished frame. "It's the last thing I've left, but I think they'll lend a trifle on it, so it shall go," said she. Forthwith I was wrapped in an old rag, and carried to a new dwelling—the pawnbroker's. The shopman seemed to know my mistress, for he laughed a coarse laugh, and said, "What, Pat! you've brought us brittle ware this time, like yourself." Then followed the haggling and chaffing. I never heard my imperfections so plainly stated before; indeed, like most people, I did not know I had them. By the shopman's account, I was old-fashioned—had a shade of green in my complexion—was likely if I stayed there to be demolished—and if I escaped that fate, I was sure to be very much in the way. Here was a change, for one who had been the favoured guest of fashionable mansions, and private councillor of my mistresses,—

"The love of ladies, and the theme of song,"

a poet says, of some one, who, perhaps, was as hollow as myself. Well! affairs had altered surely. Patty left me for about one-sixth of what pretty Mrs. Rubicand had originally given for me.

I had both ample time and means for various reflections at the pawnbroker's, for I occupied a station on a high shelf that overlooked the shop. Many of my kind were around me, and glasses of all shapes and sizes. I had not been long there, before I knew many of the customers who regularly frequented the place, and it seemed to me that their scanty wardrobes were constantly perambulating between their homes and the pawnbroker's; at first I was puzzled to know who the things actually belonged to, fancying that the pawnbroker received a premium for allowing them to be used now and then—for a brief and anxious interval, by his customers.

One thing I noticed especially; we had a large gin-palace next door, and all our customers, with very few exceptions, used to turn out of our door the instant they were served, and into the next house. Out of the hundreds that frequented our place, there were but very few who were not drunkards. And of these it might be said, their visits were few and far between. Some of them sore pressed by poverty, yet, preserving amid all, the decencies of life; and looking around with trembling anxiety, lest their visit should be discovered —poor souls! it was but seldom we saw them come for the purpose of reclaiming the articles they had left, often with bitter tears. A large class of customers were the wives of mechanics, who seemed to me little fitted to be helpmates, except in journeying the broad road to destruction. Every Monday morning these women, in parties of two or three, marched into the shop with their husbands' Sunday clothes, and sometimes those of their children. After the loan on them was procured, they would saunter into the gin-shop—then stop and gossip awhile at the corner, until, perhaps, they were thirsty: then another taste of the "fire-water," and at length they would reluctantly wend their way homeward. How many of this class through the week, brought all sorts of strange heterogeneous things— smoothing irons, cooking utensils, aprons—every trifling thing that would fetch the price of the drink, that our next door neighbour supplied. With the Saturday night came the husband's wages. Then, their visit to the gin-palaces used to precede their call upon us. Oh! the clamour, the crowding, the bawling, the scolding that was kept up from eight o'clock till twelve at night. Nothing out of Bedlam, or rather out of Pandemonium, at all resembling it. Wailing infants moaning to be taken home—their weary eyes half-closed—fevered—dirty—cross, scolded or cuffed by their virago mothers, who had little of the maternal character but the name. Poor wretched beings! I rejoice that I belong to a different kind of existence. Yet, in the midst of their improvidence and intemperance, their misery fully equalled their guilt. Every face had the gloom of angry passions, and the sharp outline of grief settled upon it. While their lives, ever in the wrong, seemed to be made up of quarrels, insult, grief, and starvation.

One thing surprised me; I saw no more of my late mistress, but one day, I heard the shopman say to a wretched girl dressed in tawdry trumpery—" What's become of your old crony—Pat?"

" Oh, indeed! she's got so low, that I'm sure she's no crony of mine," said the girl, with a toss of her empty head—" I've heard she was run'd over, and took'd on a shutter to St. Bartlemy's Hospital, but whether she's dead or alive, I don't know—nor don't care."

I had been some months in my station on the upper shelf, when, one morning in the autumn, a decent countrified-looking man entered, and made inquiries about a Bible. I knew him instantly, it was poor Patty's brother, who had come to redeem some memento of his sister. The book was found—it seemed a family relic, for there was a name written in it beside Patty's—that of her mother—the worthy man looked at it with tearful eyes, and though he made no comment, it was evident he was deeply affected. The shopman perceiving his agitation, and probably willing to turn it to account, instantly became very zealous in finding other things that had belonged to Patty, particularly such as would break or spoil. I caught his eye, and instantly I was placed on the counter; "this belonged to the same young woman, sir," said he—hoping to get rid of me." "I know it did," replied the brother, "but I would not have it if you gave it me; *that* has come to the right place, but my poor mother's Bible—her comfort in sickness, and her support in trouble; I'd have walked barefoot to London to get it from you. If my poor sister had known its worth, she'd not have lived and died an outcast. No, no! take back your decanter; you're welcome to it for me. Patty preferred it to the Bible, and I've seen the consequences."

So saying, he turned on his heel and departed; while the shopman sneeringly exclaimed—"Oh, the Methodistic fool, he's not worth minding."

A thought seemed, however, to strike his mind, for he did not return me to my place. "As she's dead, we may as well make short work of it, and sell it if possible," said he.

"But suppose any one else belonging to her comes for it, and it should be sold?"

"Why, can't we say it's broke? and we're not answerable for breakages," was the reply of this worthy individual, and forthwith, I was placed in the window, and embellished with a ticket, setting forth my good qualities and price. I stayed some months in my present position, and somehow, I thought that it was better for me to stay where I was, than to be the harbinger of sorrow and death, as I had been. I began to understand that I was a dangerous guest, likely to usurp the chief place in the esteem of the heads of the family, and to end by sending away both peace and prosperity.

One day, soon after I made these reflections, (which after all, probably arose from an empty stomach, for I have heard, that always produces melancholy); a tidy, bustling old woman, looked into the window full at me: "Surely, that thrifty-looking old dame don't intend to buy me," was my reflection, when to my surprise, in the next instant, I was handed to the counter for her inspection; I was approved, and being snugly deposited in her capacious marketing basket, off she trudged. Well! in a little time, I was unpacked, and found myself in an entirely new scene. The place I was taken to was not a dwelling-house, but a large square building, lighted with high-arched windows, and filled with seats that stretched across the middle, and down each side, while round three sides, high up and supported by pillars, were other ranges of seats, and on the fourth side was a kind of square box, ornamented with a crimson velvet cushion. There were lamps ranged round the building, and a neat lightsome look the place wore, that pleased me mightily. I had scarcely time to make these observations, when I was carried into an adjoining room, very clean, but plainly furnished, and I soon found myself consigned to a press that occupied a recess in the corner, "There," said my new mistress, placing me in it, "I hope I shan't have an accident with *you*," from which I inferred she had broken my predecessor. Two or three days passed away in darkness and solitude—the silence was so great that the ticking of the clock alone vibrated through the building. At length, early one morning, I was taken out, and being duly washed, soon after received my contents, and entered upon the duties of my situation. The good woman, strange to say, never tasted my contents; indeed, she looked somewhat crossly at me, and put me by. The next day, I heard many voices, none of them clamorous or noisy; and the sound of numerous footsteps. After a time I was brought forth, a venerable-looking man was seated at the table in that quiet room, he looked up from a large book, as I was brought near, and saying—"Ah! my poor nerves, would that I could dispense with this potion; but I am compelled to submit to my medical man, he is peremptory on this subject," saying this, he poured out a large glassful, and in truth, this gentleman seemed to take his "potion" off, with quite as much relish as if it had not been physic.

Presently after he left the room, and I heard his

voice for more than an hour, talking so beautifully about something he called "self-denial," that I quite envied him his knowledge of such a delighted theme. He returned, his face flushed and beaming; and a gentleman that accompanied him, poured out another full glass of my contents, and the good venerable man swallowed it every drop, and then uttering a deep sigh said, "I wish my health allowed me to dispense with this."

"With your labours that is impossible," said his friend. In the evening the same scene was acted again, my contents were drank with reluctance and sighs.

Two evenings in the week, I was in requisition, and sometimes the elderly and influential persons of the place, helped to lower my contents. I was often filled, and I found, that so far from the gentleman (he was called 'the minister,') whom I specially served, having his nerves benefited, they became worse, for he had to increase his dose. I continued in this place for some years, and at length I thought that the words of the minister became different in their utterance, and his style seemed dull, cold, dreamy, and indistinct; he sometimes lost the thread of his discourse, and all became entangled and perplexed. I remembered what kind of discourses he uttered when I first came, and that the place used to be then so crowded, that the forms were fetched from the room I was in, to supply seats to those who otherwise would have had to stand. Now, I could hear my master's failing voice echo and reverberate through the place, as if it were nearly empty. He drank my fluid now, with feverish eagerness, and every time he came, I thought he looked more and more thin and sallow.

One evening he came in somewhat heated and excited; he drank of me again and again. At length, when the time arrived for his commencing, he went forth with unsteady steps, and no one could complain that he was cold on that night, for I never heard him more loud, though there was something frightful in his energy; two or three persons during the discourse came in, and whispered together, looking with strangely significant glances at each other. At length he finished, and with dilated eye and quivering lips, returned to where I was deposited. He was about to quaff a second draught of my contents, when he suddenly fell prostrate on the ground in a violent fit. A medical man was sent for, who bled him, and by slow degrees, he partially recovered consciousness, a coach was called, and he was assisted to it; from that time I saw him no more. In less than a fortnight he died, it was said, of inflammation of the brain.

As the congregation had manifestly declined under his teaching, much was said about his weak state of health, but I wondered whether my contents had anything to do with it, particularly as the old pew-opener said, when dusting and putting me away, "Ah, poor dear gentleman! he died of doctors more than of disease. I'm glad I'm too poor to pay a doctor, with their stimulants and stuff, they kill as many as they cure." With this very irreverent opinion of the faculty, she locked me up.

Shortly after, a young man came to officiate. Health nerved his manly form, and high intelligence gave a grave dignity to his mien, beyond his years; while the sunshine of a soul that had felt the glow of something brighter than this earth has to bestow, irradiated his beaming face.

I heard the varied modulations of his full voice proclaiming, pleading, warning, and not in vain; Sabbath after Sabbath the place became more full. Strangers came to speak with him. A kind word, a gracious smile, he had for all; people's hearts opened beneath his influence, and soon there was a blaze of devotion, activity, and zeal, where there had been before but a cold and fitful gleam quivering in the socket.

Strange to say, I was nowise concerned in this improvement. The new minister never asked for me; I believe, never saw me, until one day he came in haste, and took a book from the vestry, his eye fell on me, and never having seen anything but kindness in his glance, judge my astonishment, when with a stern voice he exclaimed, "Remove this useless thing, I know of nothing more disgraceful than the appurtenances of intemperance and folly, lingering in the House of Prayer—take it away!"

Next day I was fastened up in a locker, in the place preparatory to removal, and I had just begun to wonder what would be the next change in my destiny, when the old pew-opener suddenly opened the locker, took me out and said, " you can have this, it will do capitally ; and I'll be bound it has never been so well employed before."

"Well," said the man to whom she offered me, "have you permission to lend it?"

" Why, bless you, our minister ordered me to take it away only yesterday, and in such a resolute way, I wish you had heard him; young as he is, I promise you he knows how to rule."

"If he did not, he would be unfit to lead others," replied the man, and I was immediately transferred to his custody. Well, I never underwent such a thorough ablution. The man seemed to think I could not be purified enough; I longed to tell him, that though I might hold strong drinks, I never imbibed any, and in this respect, had a mighty advantage over human beings. I really thought I should be shivered in the ducking and sousing the man gave me. At last, his fastidious nose was satisfied, I was pronounced completely purified. What precious liquid am I to hold now, thought I, doubtless some costly drink, fit only for the nobles of the land. " Go, fill this decanter at the filter, my dear," said the man to a blooming girl, his daughter. She instantly carried me to a stone re-

THE PROMOTION. (Page 65)

ceptacle, and I was soon filled with a cool, clear, sparkling fluid.

"There!" said the damsel, her bright blue eyes glancing gaily at me. "Now, Mr. Decanter, you're full of the best drink in the world, fine clear pure cold WATER!"

Water! I that had held rich cordials, costly liquors, choice wines, to be brought down to hold what every paltry stream and tank, and pump could supply. Who now would ever taste me? Alas! I felt that the playhouse line I heard in Mrs. Hague's dwelling, applied to me, though under a different name, "Othello's occupation 's gone," but I had not much time for these gloomy reflections. The cheerful-looking lass carried me across the road, and entered the well-known chapel, whence I had been ejected by the minister's orders, and advancing to the end before the place with the velvet cushion, she mounted some temporary steps, and placed me upon a table in the midst of a platform, where I stood between two wax candles, which were just being lighted. Soon people began to come in, and the place became very full, I was a little consoled for my loss of dignity, by the consciousness that I looked mighty well, returned the glance of the candles and sparkled as gaily as ever I had done. The minister, who had acted so unceremoniously, sat in a chair at the table where I was, and many earnest-looking men surrounded him. Then, after a little while, speaking began, and I found to my surprise, that I was now really in a very dignified position. My contents were the theme of the poet's song, the orator's eloquence, and the reasoner's arguments. Oh, I soon found out how things stood! and rejoiced in my conversion, the more particularly, as some of the fluids I had once been so unfortunate as to harbour, were stripped of their gay-coloured garments of rich brown, and rosy red, and glowing amber, and were burnt up in a flame equally blue and stinking, while a nauseous-looking pap, sickly and bitter, was all that remained of their finery.

My contents laved the lips of the speakers with really refreshing drinks, and the minister actually took notice of me, and after his beautiful concluding speech, laid his hand caressingly upon me. Many thronged to the table, and engaged to drink no more sickly compounds for the future, and all passed off well.

I knew now that I had been honoured, not degraded, by the alteration, for as the minister said, I held "a fluid that had been compounded by Almighty wisdom for, and given in abundant mercy to, man. A fluid that had flowed through the garden of Eden, and quenched the thirst of man in innocency. A fluid quaffed by the golden monarch of day himself. A fluid that encircles the universe, that hangs suspended in the clouds, that falls in genial showers, and sparkles in the gentle dew, that gives the earth its verdure, the flowers their freshness, the birds their gaiety, the cattle their vigour. A fluid that none can dispense with, though they may never have inquired its value. A fluid beyond comparison,—pure as the sky from which it descends—abundant as the earth it enriches—mild as the light that it reflects—safe as the wisdom that first poured it forth."

Well, from that time, every month I have left my hiding-place and occupied the station of honour on the platform. Many a thrilling tale I've heard, many a starting tear-drop I have witnessed, many a good resolution made in humility and piety, I've seen recorded. The people and the minister looked happy and prosperous, and all goes on well,—perhaps it was hearing the experience of others, put me upon giving mine. I shall not explain further, but finish as some of our speakers do, with an apology.

Doubtless there has been some empty bubbling, and some indistinct gurgling in my outpourings, but if my draught has proved a real refreshment to any one, why my lot is far superior to that of ordinary decanters. Little pauses have occurred between the pourings forth, like the divisions in our minister's sermons; but it's better not to drink with hot haste, but considerate leisure. With these few remarks, I put the stopper on my outpourings, called " CONCLUSION."

AN EXCELLENT JUVENILE PRESENT.

MORNING DEW-DROPS:

OR,

THE JUVENILE ABSTAINER.

BY MRS. CLARA LUCAS BALFOUR.

CONTENTS.

CHAPTER I.—THE ORIGIN AND PROGRESS, THE CAUSES AND EFFECTS, OF THE TEMPERANCE REFORMATION.

Intemperance the National Vice of England—Drinking Habits—Distilled Spirits—Dr. Clark of America—Formation of American Temperance Society—Abstinence from Spirits—John Dunlop, Esq.—Total Abstinence from all Intoxicating Liquors—First Temperance Society in Great Britain—W. Collins of Glasgow—Moderation and Abstinence—Preston—Rev. F. Beardsall—Yorkshire—Joseph Livesey's Visit to London—Achievements of Seven Men—Progress in Foreign Countries—Reclaimed Drunkards—Ireland—Members added to Christian Churches through the Temperance Reformation.

CHAPTER II.—THE TESTIMONY OF SCRIPTURE.

Israelites in the Wilderness—Elijah—Nazarites—Aaron—John the Baptist—Rechabites—Daniel—Sampson—Noah's Fall—Nabal—Ammon—Belshazzar—Herod—Solomon—Does the Bible Sanction the Use of Intoxicating Wine?—Scripture Denunciation against Intemperance—Our Duty—Influence of Example—Little Girl in Chelsea—Temperance Meeting—Admonition.

CHAPTER III.—THE TESTIMONY OF ANCIENT HISTORY.

Origin of the term "Teetotal"—Richard Turner—Egyptians the first People who made Beer—Babylonians—Cyrus a Teetotaller—Alexander the Great Killed by Intemperance—Spartan Slaves—Greeks—Roman Mothers not allowed to Taste Wine—Connexion between Intemperance and War—Lessons of Ancient Times—Ancient History should be studied by the Young.

CHAPTER IV.—THE TESTIMONY OF MODERN HISTORY.

School Libraries—Origin of Drinking Healths—Meaning of "Wassail"—Pledges—Melancholy Shipwreck of a King's Son and his Attendants—Civil War in England—Celebrated Brewery in Pimlico—Visit of the King of Denmark to England—Oliver Cromwell—Plague in London—Great Fire in London—Riots of 1788—Missions to the Heathen—Intemperate Sailors—England's Sin.

CHAPTER V.—COST OF INTEMPERANCE.

Economy—Two Schoolfellows—Miss Screw—Nine Millions of Abstainers—Fearful Expenditure of Money in Intoxicating Liquors—Ten Hundred Thousand Sovereigns a Week—Poverty of Many Families—Barley and Hops—Waste of Land and Time—Desecration of the Sabbath by the Malting Process

—Losses by Families—Wasted Mondays—Benevolent Societies—Injury to Sunday Schools—Daniel Wheeler's Visit to the South Seas—The Bread Fruit Tree—Injury to Bolabola—North American Indians—Summary of the Cost of Intemperance.

CHAPTER VI.—SELF-DENIAL.

Good Conduct—Personal and Relative Duties—What is Self-Denial?—Self-Conceit—Bad Tempers—Temperance Principle founded on Self-Denial—St. Paul's Example—Personal Moral Duties—Home Influence—Little Drops—"The Seed that his Mother Sowed"—Anecdote of a Lady—A Family Destroyed—Sunday School Festival—Effects of giving Beer to the Children—Band of Hope Children—What should be the Conduct of the Members of Bands of Hope—Courage to say "No"—Bearing to be laughed at—Pity for the Children of Poor Drunkards—The Almighty's help must be prayed for—Early Piety recommended.

CHAPTER VII.—EARLY HABITS.

Good and Bad Habits begin in Childhood—The Careless Girl—Habit of Profane Speaking—The Drunkard's Early Habits—Early Abstinence—Importance of Children being *trained up* in Temperance Principles—Firmness of a Band of Hope Boy—The Sick Child—Influence of Good or Bad Company—Danger of Drinking even "a little"—Shoemaker's Son in Hyde Park- Enlists in the Spanish Army—Heart-Broken Mother—Reformation and Useful Labours in America—Truth of the old adage, "Use is second Nature."

CHAPTER VIII.—FORCE OF EXAMPLE.

Example better than Precept—What is the Difference between Example and Precept?—Our Saviour's Example and Precepts.—Interesting Case of a Reformed Drunkard—The Duty of Christians to set a Right Example—Lord Bacon—Sir Isaac Newton—Linnæus—Dr. John Hunter—Sir Humphry Davy—Great Errors by relying upon Precept, instead of searching out the Truth—Prisons—John Howard, the Philanthropist. His written *Pledge*—The Influence of Howard's Example.

CHAPTER IX.—THE POWER OF CUSTOM.

National Customs—St. Paul's Advice—Cruel Customs among the Carribean Indians—North American Indians—New Zealanders—Circassians—Chinese Ladies—Drinking Customs—Power of *Old* Customs—Dark Ages of England—Labours of Mr. Dunlop—Drinking on Birthdays, Wedding-days, and Funerals—"Footings"—Cruelty of Workmen—A poor Rope Maker—Drinking leads to Hardness of Heart—Injurious to Apprentices and Masters—Affecting Case of a poor Widow's Son—Lord Bacon's Advice—Appeal to the Young.

CHAPTER X.—CHRISTIAN COURTESY AND BENEVOLENCE.

Lessons of Scripture—Respect due to Old Age—We must be courteous without sacrificing Principle—The little Servant Girl who would not tell a Lie—Difference between the Courtesy of the Christian, and the Courtesy of the World—The Two Cold Water Boys—Children must be Prudent as well as Zealous—What is Benevolence?—Christian Benevolence—Benevolence of the Temperance Movement—Abolition of West Indian Slavery—Slavery of Intemperance—Lamentable Death through mistaken Courtesy.

MORNING DEW DROPS—CONTENTS.

CHAPTER XI.—THE YOUNG CHEMIST'S INQUIRY.

What is it that intoxicates?—What is Alcohol?—Distillation—Arabian Alchemists—Distilleries first erected—Spoiling God's good Grain—Spirits used as Medicine only, at the first—Malt Liquors—How is Malt made?—What are Hops?—London Porter first made in 1722—Origin of the Word "Porter"—The filthy Water of the Thames used for making Porter—Singular Lawsuit by a Brewer—Adulterations by Publicans—Opium and other Narcotic Poisons—Difference between Stimulation and Strength—Wine—Alcohol in Wine—Vineyards of France, &c.—Wine without any Juice of the Grape—Sugar of Lead and other Deadly Poisons mixed with Wine—Curious Fact about the Channel Islands—Is there nourishment in Spirits, Wine, and Beer?—Interesting Experiment with the "Still."

CHAPTER XII.—THE YOUNG REASONER'S OBJECTIONS.

What is it to Reason?—Arguments used by Two Boys, for and against Temperance Principles—Uses of Horses, Swimming, Fire, &c., &c.—"A good Creature of God—Alcohol as a Medicine—The Drunkard's Children—Is Abstinence better than Moderate Drinking?—What says the Bible?—Columbus discovers America—Galileo and the Earth's Motions—Art of Printing—Robert Raikes and Sunday Schools—The Objector becomes a Total Abstainer.

CHAPTER XIII.—BIOGRAPHICAL GLEANINGS—EXAMPLES.

What is Biography?—Importance of Self-Denial—Benjamin Franklin—Franklin's noble Conduct in the Printing Office—His high Promotion in America—He discovers the Mode of Conducting Lightning—The Franklin Institutes—Dr. Johnson, Compiler of the English Dictionary—Christian Heyne of Saxony—John Wesley's Extraordinary Labours and Excellent Rules.

CHAPTER XIV.—BIOGRAPHICAL GLEANINGS—WARNINGS.

The Sufferings of William Hutton and his Mother—James Lackington's Intemperate Father—Robert Burns, the Scotch Poet—Richard Brinsley Sheridan's Intemperance—Opium—Visit to a Debtor's Prison—The Madhouse—Intemperate Mother—The Workhouse.

CHAPTER XV.—THE FEAR OF RIDICULE.

The Fear of Ridicule—The Coward—A Boarding School Boy—The Triumph of Principle—Joseph—Sampson—Treatment of our Redeemer by the Jews—The Apostles had to bear Ridicule—The Puritans—The Roundheads of the Seventeenth Century—The Society of Friends—George Whitfield and John Wesley—Methodists—John Howard—Maria Chapman and the Poor Blacks—Angelina Grimke—Lamentable Case of a Man who was afraid of being laughed at.

CHAPTER XVI.—INTEMPERANCE THE GREAT HINDRANCE TO EDUCATION.

The Present Age—Sabbath Schools—Mechanics' Institutions—Cheap Day Schools—Intemperance the Great Barrier—Habits of Drinking Parents—Duties of Children—Picture of a Middlesex Village—Visit of a Sunday-School Teacher to a Drunkard's Home—The Temperance Meeting—The Reclaimed One's Children brought to a Sunday-school—The Happy Meeting with the Teacher—The Brickmakers of West Drayton—Minister at Great Harwood—Is not the Total Abstainer the Friend of Education?

CHAPTER XVII.—THE TESTIMONY OF TRAVELLERS.

Variety of Climates—"Can People go into any Climate without Strong Drink?"—Admiral Sir John Ross—The Use of Brandy in the Cold Regions—Sir John had better Health by Abstaining, than all his Crew who used Spirits—Rev. W. Scoresby's Testimony before the House of Commons—Mrs. Jameson in Canada—Extraordinary Testimony of a Soldier—James Hogg, the Ettrick Shepherd—Affecting Anecdote of a Shepherd and his Wife—Effects of Strong Drink in Hot Climates—Use of Arrack in India by the Soldiers—Joseph Sturge—Jamaica—J. S. Buckingham, Esq.—Porters of Constantinople—James Backhouse, the African Traveller—Prisoners of War—Dr. Farre—Valuable Testimony of Thomas Shillitoe—A Poor Convict in Australia—The "little sups" given by his Father.

CHAPTER XVIII.—THE TESTIMONY OF THE STUDIOUS.

Common objection—The School Boy and his Half-pint of Porter—Testimony of the Schoolmistress—Important Statement by James Higginbotham, Esq., Surgeon, of Nottingham—Rev. W. Jay—Rev. Benjamin Parsons—Rev. Jabez Burns—Rev. Octavius Winslow—Rev. Albert Barnes—Elihu Burritt, the American Blacksmith—Thomas Clarkson, the Friend of the Slave—Miss Edgeworth—Mrs. S. C. Hall—Mrs. Ellis—Rev. W. Ellis—Joseph Livesey—Some of the wisest and best Persons are Total Abstainers.

CHAPTER XIX.—THE TESTIMONY OF THE LABORIOUS.

The Working Classes—Men at Hayle Foundry—Labourers in Richmond Park—Brickmakers at West Drayton and York—Seventeen London Smiths and Cutlers—Cornish Miners—Preston Sawyers—Haymakers at Dyrham Park and Sheriff Hutton—London Bridewell—Juvenile Depravity—Experience of Thomas Paul, who worked on the Great Western Railway.

CHAPTER XX.—A RETROSPECT.

The Value of Reading—The Young should delight in Good Books—Early Habits—Early Rising—The Necessity for seeking God's Blessing—What is the Pledge?—Value of the Pledge—Should Children be invited to Sign?—Reasons for and against the Pledge—Desire for the Welfare of the Young.

CHAPTER XXI.—OUR BANDS OF HOPE.

Bands of Hope—Their name—Influence of Hope on Human Life—Juvenile Societies in the Early Time of the Temperance Reformation—Tracts, Essays, and Advocates specially addressing the Young—Origin of Bands of Hope—Friends of the Young—Rapid Success—The Weak Things of the World Confound the Mighty—How to form Bands of Hope—Parental Approbation—Inkeeper's little Daughter—Parting Words of Advice to the Members of Bands of Hope.

CHAPTER XXII.—TRAFFIC IN INTOXICATING LIQUORS.

Retrospect of the foregoing pages—New Point of Inquiry—Differences of Opinion—The Wisdom of Law and Order—Modern Prohibitory Laws against Concealed Arms—False Dice—Lotteries—Gaming Houses—The Fate of a Gambler—Explosion—Answer to the Question, "Is Prohibition Oppression?"—Reasons in favour of a Prohibitory Law—Maine Law—Conclusion.

www.ingramcontent.com/pod-product-compliance
Lightning Source LLC
Chambersburg PA
CBHW020329090426
42735CB00009B/1465